How To *Hula*

EDITED BY
Patricia Lei Anderson Murray

PHOTOGRAPHS BY
Joe Perrone

MUTUAL

Copyright 1997
by Mutual Publishing

No part of this book may be reproduced in any form or by any
electronic or mechanical means including information storage
and retrieval devices or systems without prior written permission
from the publisher except that brief passages may be quoted
for reviews.

All rights reserved

Library of Congress Catalog
Card Number 96-79002

First Printing July 1997
Second Printing, June 1999
Third Printing, July 2001
Fourth Printing, January 2003
Fifth Printing, August 2004
5 6 7 8 9

ISBN 1-56647-099-4

Mutual Publishing
1127 11th Avenue, Mezzanine B
Honolulu, Hawaii 96816
Telephone (808) 732-1709
Fax (808) 734-4094
e-mail: mutual@mutualpublishing.com

Printed in Taiwan

$\mathcal{C}$ontents

v   Introduction

vi   How to Use This Book

vii   Basic Footwork

xi   Basic Hand Motions

xiv   The Songs

HOW TO HULA

1   *The Hukilau Song*

7   *Lovely Hula Hands*

13   *Little Brown Gal*

20   *Sweet Leilani*

26   *Keep Your Eyes on the Hands*

33   *Hawaiian Hospitality*

40   *To You, Sweetheart, Aloha*

46   *Hawaiian Wedding Song*

56   Glossary

Introduction

The words "lovely *hula* hands" bring to mind the romance of palms swaying on moon-lit beaches and waves crashing on golden sand—an enchanting notion perpetuated for decades by Hawai'i's songwriters, singers, and dancers for the millions who visit the fair islands of Hawai'i. Graceful *hula* hands, accompanied by swaying bodies adorned with fragrant flowers, have mesmerized many into believing that *hula* was only an alluring dance that steals away the heart of anyone fortunate enough to experience it.

But behind the *hula's* romance are historic visions of the sacred life-giving qualities that were so meaningful to the Hawaiians—the importance of 'ohana, family, of the 'aina, or land, and the treasures provided by them. Hawaiians danced to celebrate life and express gratitude for the abundance that was theirs. They danced for the birth of their children, for gifts of nature, and especially to honor ancestors. Hawaiians expressed life through the poetry and passion of dance. Children and loved ones were described in song and dance as rare scented flowers plucked from green mountain peaks. Dances that told of flowers and *lei* were really referring to children and loved ones.

Early Hawaiian history was once only oral history, since there was no written language until the missionaries introduced one. The *oli* or chant, along with the *hula*, were ways of telling one's life story, recounting genealogies and narrating history. Besides a major storytelling vehicle of Hawaiian life, the *hula* was also a sacred religious art form danced by a privileged and highly-regarded few, and used to teach, preserve and carry on ancient traditions for future generations.

Early visitors and newcomers to Hawai'i created their own interpretations of the *hula*. Missionaries saw the *hula* as vulgar and considered it a symptom of a degrading lifestyle lived by Hawaiians. Because of their negative view, based on a lack of understanding, the dance was banned until reinstated by King Kalakaua in the 1880s.

Within the last 25 years Hawai'i has experienced a renaissance of both *kahiko*, or ancient, and 'auana, or modern, *hula*. People of all races now join Hawaiians in *hula* festivals throughout Hawai'i, including the Merry Monarch, King Kamehameha, and Keiki *Hula*. New festivals are emerging in Hawai'i, as well as on the mainland and even in countries as far away as Japan.

The *hula's* alluring magic continues to endure. *How to Hula* has been created to help people of all ages to learn to dance and enjoy the *hula*. The songs included are visitor's favorites comprised of *hapa haole* songs, written originally in English. Popular during the thirties, forties and fifties, they are still requested today.

So get ready to feel beautiful, and be a part of the rain, wind, and warm sun of Hawai'i as you learn to use your lovely *hula* hands with grace. Discover a new way to celebrate life—learn to dance the *hula*!

Patricia Lei Anderson Murray

How to use this book

This book uses step-by-step photographs and written instructions to teach the *hula*. The photographs show the main positions, while the captions provide the song lyrics, the footwork, and hand motions.

Dancers who use this book will find it very worthwhile to learn basic foot movements first, then fit the hand motions into the rhythm. In many cases, the dance is best learned by phrases.

For example, when doing "Lovely Hula Hands," review steps 1, 2, and 3 and see how they flow together from one motion to another. Learn the footwork first, without trying the hands. Then work through the hand movements. Finally, put both the hands and feet together. Learning by phrases will help you remember the story you are telling.

So, take your time with each dance. Feel the poetry of the movements and how they relate to the lyrics. And, above all, have fun.

Basic footwork

To dance the *hula*, you must have some idea of the basic steps and hand motions. Grace and coordination come with practice and desire. Good dancers feel the rhythm of the music and move naturally with it. Shoulders should be relaxed, back straight, and knees slightly bent, arms and fingers moving gracefully.

Here is a footwork glossary of basic foot patterns generally used in hula. Note that not all of the movements will be used in each song. We have chosen to use the simplest patterns.

kaholo: The most important *hula* step is the *kaholo*, (once referred to as the "vamp"). *Kaholo* is the most often used step, whether it be side to side, front to back, or diagonally. A *kaholo* is more of a sliding step, rather than lifting the foot as you move.

kaholo right: Right foot takes a short step to the right. Bring left foot beside the right. Take another step to the right, then bring the left foot next to it and hold.
Right, left, right, hold. 4 counts.

Kaholo Right

![Kaholo Right foot pattern diagram showing feet positions numbered 2, 1, 4, 3 with arrows pointing right from Start]

Start

kaholo left: Left foot takes a short step to the left. Right foot follows. The pattern is repeated on the left in the same manner as it was on the right.
Left, right, left, hold. 4 counts.

Kaholo Left

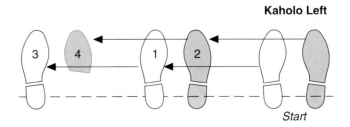

Start

ka'o: Sway hips by shifting weight to the right side and lifting left heel. Then shift weight to the left side and lift right heel. Sways are usually done in 2 or 4 counts.

Ka'o

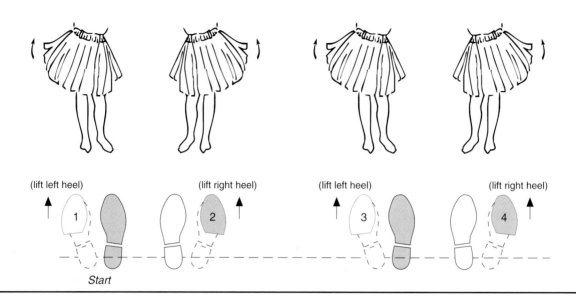

(lift left heel)   (lift right heel)   (lift left heel)   (lift right heel)

Start

lele: Step right, then left, either forward or back. 2 counts each side.

lele forward

lele back
Start

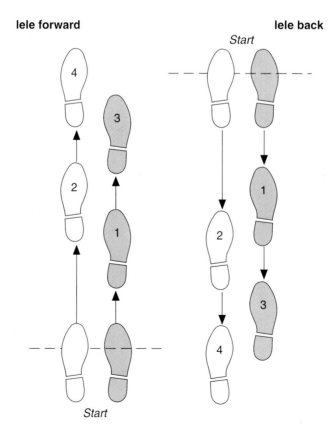

Start

hela: Point right foot forward, bring back, then point left foot forward, then bring back. *Hela* can be done in 2 or 4 counts.

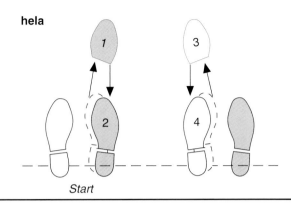

hela

Start

'ami: Right—rotate hips counterclockwise, one rotation for each count. Left—rotate hips clockwise. Bent knees make the *'ami* easier.

'ami

Right   *Left*

around the island: Step on the right foot. Do one complete *'ami*. Pivot on the left foot. Repeat three more *'ami* while moving in a circle to face front again.

around the island

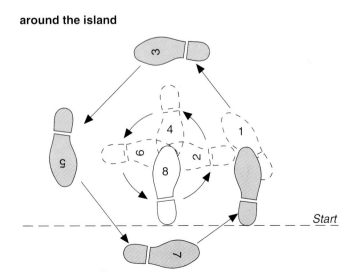

Start

holoholo: Slide 8 steps to the right (four counts), then 8 steps to the left.

holoholo right

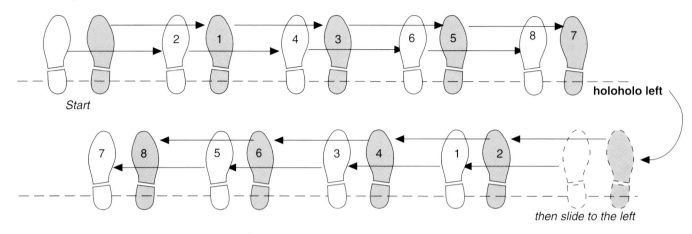

holoholo left

then slide to the left

'uwehe: Step on right foot, then lift both heels and push knees slightly apart. Step left, repeat same movements on the left. Shoulders should not move when heels are lifted. 2 counts for each *'uwehe*.

'uwehe

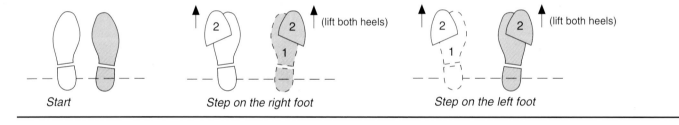

---

lele 'uwehe: Step to right, brush foot forward, bring back and lift heels. Step left, repeat same steps, going left.

lele 'uwehe

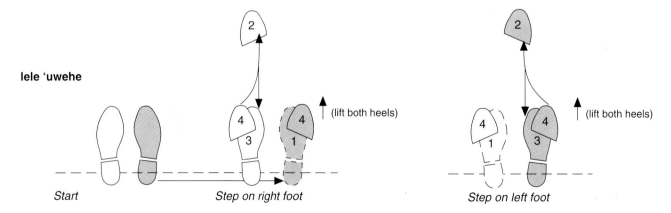

Basic hand motions

Graceful hands tell the story, but the dance is most beautiful when it is enjoyed by the dancer as well as the audience. A good dancer visualizes what she describes—the mountains are cool and high, the flowers fresh and fragrant—when she knows her story, her *hula* can be truly enjoyed by all. Here are some basic *hula* hand motions.

Let's go to the *ocean*

hands gently beat up and down showing the rhythm of the waves

And watch the *tide roll in*

hands continually roll over each other to show the rolling sea

The swaying *palms*

left arm becomes the land, right arm and fingers sway showing a waving palm

And the swirling *winds*.

left hand forward while right hand circles twice over head

The rising *sun*

start at the knees, both hands part and rise above the head to shape the sun

The *clouds* rolling by

hands continue to roll over head moving from one side to the other

The colors of the *rainbow*

palms meet at the left…right hand lifts and shapes an arching rainbow

And the *stars* in the sky.

both hands meet over head; two fingers of each hand cross to shape the stars

Let's go to the *mountains*

right hand higher than the left shaping mountain cliffs

The *valleys* low

right hand up and left hand gracefully moving down to feet, for valley

I'll sing you a *song*

hand gracefully gesturing at mouth for song

Of *long ago*.

hands cross at chest, then open to extend out

I'll string you a *lei*

left hand up holding a flower, right hand using a needle to string a lei

For you to *wear*

both hands above head, coming down at neck to show the wearing of a lei

And gather *flowers*

finger tips closed and pointing downward; wrists turn upward as flower blooms

For your *hair*.

*hands gesturing to the left to
show flowers in the hair*

This is the *story*

*hands at mouth to tell story or
to sing a song*

Our *hands* can tell

*hands at chest level and gracefully
alternating, one on top the other*

Of our *island home*

*palms inward at waist, extend side ways,
wrists turn, palms face outward, fingers come
together to shape an island*

That we *love* so well.

*hands cross at chest to show
embracing love*

The Songs

The Hukilau Song

by Jack Owens, Copyright renewed 1976 and assigned to Owens-Kemp Music Co. (ASCAP)

Oh, we're going to a hukilau,
A huki, huki, huki, huki, hukilau.

Everybody loves a hukilau,
Where the laulau is the kaukau
    at the hukilau.

We throw our nets out into the sea,
And all the 'ama'ama come
    swimming to me.

Oh, we're going to a hukilau,
Huki, huki, huki, huki, hukilau.

What a beautiful day for fishing,
The old Hawaiian way,
And the hukilau nets are swishing,
Down in old La'ie Bay.

Oh, we're going to a hukilau,
Huki, huki, huki, huki, hukilau.

Lovely Hula Hands

Written by Alex Anderson, Copyright ©1940 PolyGram International Publishing, Inc.

Lovely hula hands,
Graceful as the birds in motion,
Gliding like the gulls over
    the ocean,
Lovely hula hands,
Kou lima nani e.

Lovely hula hands,
Telling of the rain in the valley,
And the swirling winds over
    the pali,
Lovely hula hands,
Kou lima nani e.

I can feel the soft caresses
    of your hula hands,
Your lovely hula hands.

Every little move expresses
    so I'll understand,
All the tender meaning
    of your hula hands,
Fingertips that say, "Aloha,"
Say to me again, "I love you,"
Lovely hula hands,
Kou lima nani e.

Little Brown Gal

by Johnny Noble, Lee Wood and Don McDiarmid
©Copyright 1935 by Bourne Co.

It's not the islands fair
    that are calling to me,
Not the balmy air
    not the tropical sea,
But it's a little brown gal,
    in a little grass skirt,
In a little grass shack, in Hawaii.

It isn't Waikiki
    nor Kamehameha's pali,
Not the beach boys free,
    with their ho'omalimali,
It's a little brown gal,
    in a little grass skirt,
In a little grass shack in Hawaii.

Through that island wonderland,
She's broken all the kane's hearts.
It's not hard to understand,
For that wahine is a gal of parts.

I'll be leaving soon,
    but the thrill I'll enjoy,
Is not the island moon,
    or the fish and the poi,
It's just a little brown gal,
    in a little grass skirt,
In a little grass shack in Hawaii.

Sweet Leilani

by Harry Owens, Copyright 1935 Royal Music Publisher

Sweet Leilani, heavenly flower,
Nature fashioned roses kissed
    with dew,
And then she placed them
    in a bower,
It was the start of you.

Sweet Leilani, heavenly flower,
I dreamed of paradise for two,
You are my paradise completed,
You are my dreams come true.

Sweet Leilani, heavenly flower,
Tropic skies are jealous
    as they shine,
I think they're jealous
    of your blue eyes,
Jealous because you're mine.

Sweet Leilani, heavenly flower,
I dreamed of paradise for two,
You are my paradise completed,
You are my dreams come true.

Keep Your Eyes on the Hands

by Tony Todaro & Mary Johnston, © 1955-1956 Criterion Music Corp./So. Sea Music (ASCAP) © Renewed 1983 Criterion Music Corp./So. Sea Music (ASCAP)

Whenever you're watching
    a hula girl dance,
You gotta be careful,
You're tempting romance,
Don't keep your eyes on her hips,
Her naughty hula hips,
Keep your eyes on her hands.

Remember she's telling a story
    to you,
Her opu is swaying,
But don't watch the view,
Don't concentrate on that swing,
It doesn't mean a thing,
Just keep your eyes on her hands.

And when she goes around
   the island,
Swaying hips so tantalizing,
Keep your eyes where they
   belong,
And when her grass skirt
   goes a swishing,
Keep your head and don't go
   wishing,
That you'd like to mow the lawn.

Your eyes are revealing,
You're fooling no one,
No use in concealing,
We're having some fun,
But if you're too young to date,
Or over ninety-eight,
Keep your eyes on the hands.

(They tell the story.)

Just keep your eyes on the hands.

Hawaiian Hospitality

by Harry Owens and Ray Kinney. Copyright 1938 Royal Music Publisher

Along the beach at Waikiki,
A fair wahine is waiting for me,
With her dark eyes and
   lovable charms,
And very sweet Hawaiian
   hospitality.

Beneath the moon we stroll along,
And life is just like a beautiful
   song,
When she whispers, "Come into
   my arms,"

It's just the old Hawaiian
   hospitality.

And though my heart may sob
   to "Aloha" when I sail away,
How my heart will throb to the
   thought of coming back some day.
And when my dreams of love
   come true,
There will be 'okolehao for two,
A little wela ka hao might do.
It's just the old Hawaiian
   hospitality.

To You, Sweetheart, Aloha

by Harry Owens. Copyright 1937 Royal Music Publisher

To you, sweetheart, aloha,
Aloha from the bottom
   of my heart.
Keep the smile on your lips,
Brush the tears from your eye.
One more aloha,
Then it's time for good bye.

To you, sweetheart, aloha,
In dreams I'll be with you,
   dear, tonight,
And I'll pray for that day when
We two will meet again.
Until then, sweetheart, aloha.

Hawaiian Wedding Song

by Al Hoffman, Dick Manning and Charles E. King. Copyright © 1926, 1958 (Renewed) by Charles E. King Music Co., MCA Music Publishing, a div. of MCA Inc. & Al Hoffman Songs, Inc., c/o Music Sales Corporation

This is the moment I've waited for,
I can hear my heart singing,
Soon bells will be ringing.

This is the moment of sweet aloha,
I will love you longer than forever,
Promise me that you will leave
   me never.

Here and now, dear,
All my love I vow, dear,
I will love you longer than forever,
Promise me that you will leave
   me never.

Now that we are one,
Clouds won't hide the sun,
Blue skies of Hawaii smile
   on this our wedding day!

I do love you,
With all my heart.

Here and now, dear,
All my love I vow, dear.
I will love you longer than forever,
Promise me that you will
   leave me never.

Now that we are one
Clouds won't hide the sun
Blue skies of Hawaii smile
   on this our wedding day!
I do love you,
With all my heart.
With all my heart.

The Hukilau Song

by Jack Owens

The old Hawaiian way of fishing is to lay out the long nets in the ocean in the evening, and in the morning the whole community would come and help pull the nets in. This fun song tells of this favorite way of fishing–the *hukilau*.

1 **Oh, we're going**
Kaholo right.
Right thumb hitching,
left hand on hip.

2 **to a hukilau**
Kaholo left. Pull nets two times
from the right to the left.

3 **a huki, huki, huki, huki,**
Kaholo right.
Pull two times left to the right.
hukilau
Kaholo left. Pulling nets two times
from right to left.

4 **Everybody**
Kaholo right. Palms up and out.

5 **loves a hukilau**
Kaholo left. Pull nets two times
from the right to left.

6 **Where the laulau**
Ka'o right.
Left palm up, dip right two fingers
into the palm.

7 **is the kaukau**
Ka'o left.
Bring same fingers to mouth
to taste the food.

8 **at the hukilau**
Kaholo right. Pull nets two times
left to two times right.

9 **We throw our nets**
Kaholo left.
Throw from right shoulder
over to ocean on left.

13 **Oh, we're going**
Kaholo right.
Right thumb hitching,
Left hand on hip.
(same as step 1)

14 **to a hukilau**
Kaholo left. Pull nets two times
from the right to the left.
(same as step 2)

15 **a huki, huki, huki,**
Kaholo right.
Pull nets two times from the left
to right.
hukilau
Kaholo left.
Pull nets two times from the right
to the left.
(same as step 3)

10 **out into the sea**
Kaholo right.
Ocean motion.

11 **And all the 'ama 'ama**
Ka'o right, left.
Right hand over left
with thumbs moving as fins.

12 **come swimming to me**
Four small ka'o, dipping.
Hands the same.

16 **What a beautiful day**
Kaholo right.
Hands open above head.

17 **for fishing**
Kaholo left.
Throw nets from right shoulder
to ocean on left.

18 **the old Hawaiian way**
Ka'o four times.
Hands from self out.

19 **And the hukilau nets are swish-ing**
Kaholo right, left.
Swish hands twice on the left,
then on right.

20 **down in old La'ie Bay**
Side kaholo stepping on the right.
Left hand up, right palm up,
at waist, turn then reverse motion,
and repeat.

21 **Oh, we're going**
Kaholo right.
Right thumb hitching,
left hand on hip.
(same as step 1)

25 **loves a hukilau**
Kaholo left. Pull nets two times
from the right to the left.
(same as step 5)

26 **Where the laulau**
Ka'o right.
Left palm up, dip right two fingers
into the palm.
(same as step 6)

27 **is the kaukau**
Ka'o left.
Bring same fingers to mouth
to taste the food.
(same as step 7)

22 **to a hukilau**
Kaholo left. Pull nets two times from the right to the left.
(same as step 2)

23 **a huki, huki, huki, huki,**
Kaholo right.
Pull two times from the left to the right.
hukilau
Kaholo left. Then pull nets two times from the right to the left.
(same as step 3)

24 **Everybody**
Kaholo right. Palms up and out.
(same as step 4)

28 **at the hukilau**
Kaholo right. Pull left to right.
(same as step 8)

29 **We throw our nets**
Kaholo left.
Throw from right shoulder over to ocean on left.
(same as step 9)

30 **out into the sea**
Kaholo right.
Ocean motion.
(same as step 10)

31 **And all the 'ama 'ama**
Ka'o right, left.
Right hand over left
with thumbs moving as fins.

(same as step 11)

32 **come swimming to me**
Four small ka'o, dipping.
Hands the same.

(same as step 12)

33 **Oh, we're going**
Kaholo right.
Right thumb hitching,
left on hip.

(same as step 1)

34 **to a hukilau**
Kaholo left. Pull nets two times
from the right to the left

(same as step 2)

35 **a huki, huki, huki,**
Kaholo right.
huki, huki, huki,
Kaholo left.
huki, huki, huki...
Kaholo right.

(same as step 3)

36 **hukilau**
On final hukilau—step back
with left foot, point right foot.
Hands come together and
extend over pointed foot.
Bow from waist.

Lovely Hula Hands
by R. Alex Anderson

Lovely Hula Hands" is one of the most romantic hulas and quite easy to learn. The motions let you glide as a seagull, tell of rain and swirling winds and feel the caress of love all in one dance.

8

1 **Lovely hula hands**
Kaholo right.
Gracefully extend hands
upward right, palms out.
(hula hands position)

2 **Graceful as the birds in**
Kaholo left.
Repeat motions on the left.

3 **motion**
Kaholo right.
Finger tips on shoulders, then
extended in a wing motion.
Kaholo left.
Repeat motions on the left.

7 **Kou lima nani e**
Ka'o right, then left.
Repeat same hands on the left.

8 **Lovely hula hands**
Kaholo right.
Hands at hula position to the
right.

9 **Telling of the rain**
Kaholo left.
Both hands swooping upward
from the right to the left.

4 **Gliding like the gulls**
Ka'o right to left.
Stay in winged position,
dipping in sway.

5 **over the ocean**
Kaholo right.
Hands rolling one over the other
as the waves do.

6 **Lovely Hula Hands**
Kaholo left.
Gracefully extend hands
upward right, palms out.
(hula hands position)

10 **in the valley**
Kaholo right.
Sprinkling raindrops down from
the left to the right.
Kaholo left.
Repeat motions from right to left.

11 **And the swirling winds**
Kaholo right.
Left hand out,
right hand circling head 2 times

12 **over the pali**
Kaholo left.
Left hand up,
right fingers touching left palm.

13 **Lovely hula hands**
Kaholo right, hula hands position.

14 **Kou lima nani e**
Kaholo left.
Hands upward on the left,
palms facing you.

15 **I can feel the soft caresses**
Ka'o four counts from right to
left.
Hands crossed at chest,
fingers moving up and down
gently along arms.

19 **expresses**
'Ami left two counts.
Switch hands and repeat motion.
Looking over left shoulder.

20 **So I'll understand**
Kaholo right.
Right index finger at temple,
left index finger at right elbow.

21 **All the tender meaning**
Kaholo left.
Fold palms up then open up front.

16 **'of your hula hands**
Kaholo right.
Hula hands position.

17 **Your lovely hula hands**
Kaholo Left. Hula hands position.

18 **Every little move**
'Ami right two counts.
Left hand on hip,
right hand at chest looking over
right shoulder.

22 **of your hula hands**
Kaholo right.
Hula hands position.

23 **Fingertips that say**
Ka'o left, right.
Hands gracefully moving left over
right, right over left.

24 **Aloha**
Kaholo left.
Hands from mouth out.
Kaholo right.
Hands open.

12

25 **Say to me again**
Ka'o left, right.
Hands from mouth to self.

26 **'I love you**
Kaholo left.
Hands come from sides
to cross and embrace.

27 **Lovely hula hands**
Kaholo right.
Hula hands position.

28 **Kou lima nani e**
Step back on left foot,
point right foot.
Hands upward on left, palms up
facing outward.
Bow—open hands to shoulder
level, palms down, keep foot in
same position —bow.

Little Brown Gal

Words and music by Lee Wood, Don McDiarmid and Johnny Noble

A great favorite, this simple hula about a Hawaiian sweetheart is among the first requested at any gathering. The motions tell the story well, and *kama'aina* find this a great one to teach to *malihini* friends.

14

1 **It's not the islands fair**
Kaholo right.
Left hand up,
right hand, palm down
moving across the body
from left to right.

2 **that are calling to me**
Kaholo left.
Left hand to mouth,
right hand extended forward,
then both hands to me.

3 **Not the balmy air**
Kaholo right.
Left hand out, right hand circling
two times over head.

7 **in a little grass shack**
Kaholo right.
Form a roof with hands.

8 **in Hawaii**
Kaholo left.
Right hand up. Left hand palm
down moving across the body
from right to left.

9 **It isn't Waikiki**
Kaholo right.
Ocean motion.

4 **not the tropical sea**
Kaholo left.
Ocean motion.

5 **It's a little brown gal**
Kaholo right.
From overhead, outline self.

6 **in a little grass skirt**
Kaholo left.
Swish skirt with both hands.

10 **nor Kamehameha's pali**
Kaholo left.
Hands form cliffs.

11 **Not the beach boys free**
Step forward right once,
left once. Point right hand
first then left.

12 **with their hoʻomalimali**
ʻAmi 2 times.
Cross arms and stroke upper
arms with fingers.

13 **It's a little brown gal**
Kaholo right.
From overhead, outline self.
(same as step 5)

14 **in a little grass skirt**
Kaholo left.
Swish skirt with both hands.
(same as step 6)

15 **in a little grass shack**
Kaholo right.
Form a roof with hands.
(same as step 7)

19 **wonderland**
Last of four steps.
Continue alternate positions.

20 **She's broken all the kane's**
Kaholo right.
Clench fists by heart
to show something being
broken two times.

21 **hearts**
Kaholo left.
Turn palms to face each other.

16 **in Hawaii**
Kaholo left.
Right hand up. Left hand palm
down moving across the body
from right to left.
(same as step 8)

17 **Through that**
Steps 17 through 19
form one motion. Take four steps
in "Around the Island" motion,
starting with right foot.
Point left hand up.

18 **island**
Second of four steps.
Alternate hand positions.

22 **It's not hard**
Kaholo right.
Left hand on hip, right hand
forward shaking finger two times.

23 **to understand**
Kaholo Left.
Right index finger at temple,
left index at right elbow.

24 **For that**
Step forward right foot.
At the same time point with right
hand, then clap.

25 **wahine is a**
Step forward left foot.
Point with left hand, then clap.

26 **gal of parts**
Ka'o two times.
From over head, outline self.

27 **I'll be leaving soon**
Kaholo right.
Right hand up,
left hand extended to left.

31 **It's a little brown gal**
Kaholo right.
From overhead, outline self.
(same as step 5)

32 **in a little grass skirt**
Kaholo left.
Swish skirt with both hands.
(same as step 6)

33 **in a little grass shack**
Kaholo right.
Form a roof with hands.
(same as step 7)

28 **but the thrill I'll enjoy**
Kaholo left.
Embrace motion.

29 **is not the island moon**
Kaholo right.
Hands start to shape the moon
from knees and rise.

30 **or the fish and the poi**
Kaholo left.
Left hand palm up,
right hand two fingers dip into
left palm, then to mouth.

34 **in Hawaii**
Kaholo left.
Right hand up. Left hand palm
down moving across the body
from right to left.
(same as step 8)

35 **Pau.**
Point right foot forward, hands
meet, head slightly bowed.

Sweet Leilani

by Harry Owens

Sweet Leilani was symbolic of beauty, grace and paradise come true. She caused a stir, however, because of her blue eyes and therein lies the intrigue of this favorite song.

1 **Sweet Leilani**
Ka'o right, left.
Hands at head then gracefully
move down to hips.

2 **heavenly flower**
Point right foot.
Hands pick flower, and hold up
on right side.

3 **Nature fashioned roses kissed
with dew**
Kaholo right.
Hands sprinkling rain from right
down to left.
Kaholo left.
Repeat rain from left to right.

4 **and then she placed them
in a bower**
Kaholo right.
Left hand up, right hand palm
down moving from left to right.
Kaholo left.
Repeat motion on opposite side.

5 **It was the start of you**
Kaholo right.
Hands from self, forward,
palms up.
Kaholo left.
Pointing to left, palms down,
motioning "you".

6 **Sweet Leilani**
Ka'o right, left.
Hands at head then gracefully
move down to hips.

22

7 **heavenly flower**
Kaholo right.
Hands pick flower and shape bud.

8 **I dreamed of paradise**
Kaholo left.
Palms together at right temple for "dreamed."

9 **for two**
Kaholo right.
Two fingers showing with right hand, left hand on hip.

13 **Sweet Leilani**
Ka'o right, left.
Hands at head then gracefully move to hips.

14 **heavenly flower**
Kaholo right.
Hands pick flower and shape bud.

15 **Tropic skies are jealous as they shine**
Kaholo left.
Hands move above head from right to left for rolling clouds.
Kaholo right.
Continue motion.

10 **You are my paradise**
Ka'o left, right.
Hands pointing to right.

11 **completed**
Kaholo left.
Open hands cross over chest
in embrace.

12 **You are my dreams come true**
Kaholo right.
Hands in dream position.
Kaholo left.
Hands open from self and out.

16 **I think they're jealous of your**
Hela left, right.
Think motion.

17 **blue eyes**
Hela left, right.
Motion to eyes.

18 **jealous because you're mine**
Kaholo left.
Right hand on hip, left arm over
chest, looking over left shoulder.
Ka'o right, left.
Repeat motion on opposite side.

19 **Sweet Leilani**
Ka'o right, left.
Hands at head then gracefully
move to hips.

20 **heavenly flower**
Kaholo right.
Hands pick flower and shape bud.

21 **I dreamed of paradise**
Kaholo left.
Hands in dream position.

25 **you are my dreams**
Kaholo right.
Hands at dream position.

26 **come true**
Step back on left foot,
point right foot…
Hands come from self forward
and open, palms up,
palms down…

27 …and bow.

22 **for two**
Ka'o right, left.
Two fingers, right hand,
left hand on hip.

23 **You are my paradise**
Kaholo right.
Hands pointing to right.

24 **completed**
Kaholo left.
Hands open and cross over chest
in embrace.

Keep Your Eyes on the Hands

by Tony Todaro and Mary Johnston

Here's a fun hula that describes the temptation of watching the wrong thing! The hands tell the story, but the eyes easily wander and the message is, "If you're too young to date, or over ninety-eight... Auwe! Just keep your eyes on the hands."

1 **Whenever you're watching**
Kaholo right.
Left hand to eyes, right hands
scan from eyes, out.

2 **a hula girl dance**
Kaholo left.
Hands in hula position on left.

3 **You gotta be careful**
Kaholo right.
Left hand on hip, right index
finger shaking two times.

4 **You're tempting romance**
Kaholo left.
Hands embrace.

5 **Don't keep your eyes on her
hips**
'Ami right two times.
Hands first on eyes then on hips.

6 **Her naughty hula hips**
'Ami right two more times.
Right hand at chest, left on hip.

7 **Just keep your eyes**
Kaholo right.
Hands to eyes.

8 **on her hands**
Kaholo left.
Hand hands up at left.

9 **Remember she's telling a story**
Kaholo right.
Hands at mouth and out.

13 **Don't concentrate on that swing, it doesn't mean a thing**
'Ami two times to the right.
Right arm at chest, left at hip.
'Ami two times to the left.
With arms, repeat motion.

14 **Just keep your eyes**
Kaholo right.
Hands at eyes.

15 **on her hands**
Kaholo left.
Hands held up at right.

10 **to you**
Kaholo left.
Point.

11 **Her opu is swaying**
Ka'o right, left.
Hands at opu.

12 **But don't watch the view**
Ka'o left, right. Right index finger
shaking two times.

16 **And when she goes around
the island, swaying hips so
tantalizing**
Step off on right foot and pivot
on left to go around in a circle…

…'ami four times, right arm at the
chest, looking over right shoulder,
then over left shoulder.

17 **keep your eyes where they belong**
Kaholo right, left.
Hands at eyes, palms in…

…then out.

18 **And when her grass skirt goes a-swishing**
Kaholo right.
Swish skirt.

22 **Your eyes are revealing, you're fooling no one**
Kaholo left, right hands at eyes, palms in,…

…then out.

23 **No use in concealing**
Side kaholo left.
Right arm at chest, looking over right shoulder.

19 **Keep your head and don't go wishing**
Kaholo left.
Left hand on hip, right index finger shaking two times.

20 **that you'd like to**
Ka'o right, left.
Hands on mower handle pushing in and out.

21 **mow the lawn**
Kaholo right.
Hands repeat mowing motion two times.

24 **we're having some fun**
Side kaholo right. Switch arms repeat motion, look over left shoulder.

25 **But if you're too young to date**
Kaholo left.
Arms in cradle position.

26 **'or over ninety-eight**
Step right, then left with double
sway on each step, right hand as if
on cane, left hand on hip.

Tag: **Just keep your eyes**
Kaholo right, left.
Hands in step 14.

on the hands
Step right, left, right, left, turning in
a circle. Left hand up, right hand
at waist, alternating four times.
On fourth step point right foot
forward, keep right hand up,
open, left hand out and bow.

Hawaiian Hospitality
Words and music by Harry Owens and Ray Kinney

The charms of a beautiful Hawaiian woman are described in this happy hula. Moments spent together were precious memories and he longed for the thought of coming back some day.

1 **Along the Beach**
Step forward right foot.
Hands to left, palms down.

2 **At Wai...**
Step left.
Repeat hands to the right.

3 **...kiki**
Kaholo right.
Ocean motion.

7 **and lovable charms**
Kaholo left.
Embrace motion.

8 **and very sweet**
'Ami, right two times.
Right arm at chest,
left hand at hip.

9 **Hawaiian Hospitality**
'Ami, left two times.
Alternate arms of last motion.

4 **A fair wahine is waiting**
Kaholo left.
From overhead, outline self.

5 **for me**
Ka'o two times.
Right index finger at temple, left index at right elbow

6 **With her dark eyes**
Kaholo right.
Hands at eyes.
Palms in, then out.

10 **Beneath the moon we stroll along**
Kaholo right, then left.
Shape moon starting at knees and rise.

11 **And life is just like a beautiful**
Kaholo right.
Arms reach out in front.

12 **song**
Kaholo left.
Hands mouth out.

13 **When she whispers**
Ka'o two times.
Right hand up, left index finger at
lips, then out.

14 **Come into my arms**
Ka'o two times.
Embrace motion.

15 **It's just the old Hawaiian
Hospitality**
'Ami right twice, then left twice.
Right arm at chest, left arm on
hip.

18 **Aloha**
Kaholo forward right.
Mouth out.

19 **When I sail away**
Kaholo forward left.
Fingertips shape a boat and dip in
water two times.

20 **How my heart**
Ka'o two times.
Turn palms to face each other.

left arm at chest, right on hip.

16 **And though my heart**
Kaholo right.
Turn palms to face each other.

17 **may sob to**
Kaholo left.
Reverse palms gracefully.

21 **will throb to the thought**
Ka'o two times.
Reverse palms gracefully.

22 **of coming back**
Step back with right foot.
Beckon on left.

Step back with left foot.
Beckon on right.

23 **some day**
Kaholo right forward.
Hands out.

24 **And when my dreams**
Ka'o once.
Dream motion.

25 **of love**
Ka'o once.
Embrace motion.

29 **A little wela…**
Kaholo left. On first step to the
left, slap skirt.

30 **ka…**
On second step which is right
foot, clap hands.

31 **hao**
On third step which is left foot,
click fingers.

26 **come true**
Kaholo left.
Extend hands forward and open.

27 **There will be okolehao**
Ka'o two times.
Dip and arms sweep up to hold drink to lips.

28 **for two**
Kaholo right.
Right hands holds up two fingers, left on hip.

32 **might do**
Kaholo right.
Hands open out front.

33 **It's just the old Hawaiian Hospitality**
Ami two times to the right, then 'ami two times to the left.

34 Step back on the left foot. Right foot pointed and bow.

To You, Sweetheart, Aloha

Words and music by Harry Owens

Imagine a cruise ship pulling away from the dock and strains of "To You, Sweetheart, Aloha" playing in the breeze. This is a memory not easily forgotten, and a "goodbye" that only this hula can express.

1 **To you**
Kaholo right.
Hands pointing to right.

2 **sweetheart**
Kaholo left.
Cross arms at chest, looking over
left shoulder.

3 **aloha**
Kaholo right.
Left hand up, right hand from
mouth out to right.
Kaholo left.
Repeat opposite motion on left.

4 **Aloha**
Kaholo right.
Hands from self out.

5 **from the bottom of my**
Kaholo left.
Continue motion until hands
are outstretched.

6 **heart**
Ka'o for 4 counts.
Right, left, right, left.
Hands roll at heart.

7 **Keep the smile on your**
Kaholo right.
Hands to smile, palms in.

8 **lips**
Kaholo left.
Turn hands outward at face.

9 **Brush the tears from your**
Kaholo right.
Gently brush tears.

13 **Then it's time for good bye**
Kaholo right.
Right arm over chest, left on hip.
Kaholo left.
Repeat motion on opposite side.

14 **To you,**
Kaholo right.
Hands pointing to right
(same as step 1)

15 **sweetheart,**
Kaholo left.
Cross arms at chest, looking over
left shoulder.
(same as step 2)

10 **eye**
Kaholo left.
Palms out at eyes.

11 **One more**
Kaholo right.
Left hand on hip, right hand pointing.

12 **aloha**
Kaholo left.
Arms cross for embrace.

16 **aloha**
Kaholo right.
Left hand up, right hand from mouth out to right.
Kaholo left.
Repeat opposite motion on left.
(same as step 3)

17 **In dreams I'll be with you dear**
Ka'o four counts.
Right, left, right, left.
Slowly come to dream position at right temple.

18 **tonight**
Kaholo right, left.
Hands over head, gently cross, then open.

19 **And I'll pray for that day**
Kaholo right.
Prayer position.

20 **when**
Kaholo left.
Hands open from self forward.

23 **Until then**
Kaholo left.
Hands from self forward and
open.

24 **sweetheart**
Kaholo right.
Hands open and crossing to
embrace.

21 **We two will meet**
Ka'o right, left.
Two fingers on right hand, left
hand on hip.

22 **again**
Kaholo right.
Hands clasp up front.

25 **aloha**
Kaholo right.
Left hand up, right hand from
mouth out to right

26 Step back on left foot,
hands open, palms down,
and bow.

The Hawaiian Wedding Song

by Al Hoffman, Dick Manning and Charles E. King

The "Hawaiian Wedding Song" is such a special part of an island wedding. You can make your wedding day special by learning this hula and dancing it for your sweetheart. Make a dream come true with the "Hawaiian Wedding Song."

1 **This is**
Kaholo right.
Palms up from self forward.

2 **the moment**
Ka'o left, right
Palms down, together then out.

3 **I've waited for**
Kaholo left.
Left hand at chest,
right hand down to side,
looking over right shoulder.
Kaholo right.
Reverse hands,
looking over the left shoulder.

4 **I can hear**
Kaholo left.
Left hand opened at ear, right
hand moving from ear out.

5 **my heart singing**
Ka'o right, left.
Hands roll twice at the heart.

6 **Soon bells**
Step right, then left in a circle.
Left hand up, right hand at chest,
then alternate hands in bell
ringing motion.

7 **will be ringing**
…ringing bells for four counts.

8 **This is**
Kaholo right.
Palms up from self forward.

9 **the moment**
Kaholo left.
Palms down, together then out.

13 **Promise me that you will leave me**
Ka'o right, left.
Hands from self,
then out to right side.

14 **never**
Kaholo right.
Left hand on hip,
right finger gesturing "never."

15 **Here and**
Lele left, then lele right.
Right hand to chest,
left hand forward,
alternate hands on lele.

10 **of sweet aloha**
Ka'o four counts, right to left.
Arms out, cross to embrace.

11 **I will love you longer**
Kaholo right.
Hands to self,
then cross to embrace.

12 **than forever**
Kaholo left.
Hands scoop down, cross,
and open above head.

16 **how dear**
Kaholo left.
Open hands, palms up.

17 **All my love I vow dear**
'Ami four counts.
Hands outstretched and crossing
to embrace.

18 **I will love you longer**
Kaholo right.
Hands to self,
then cross to embrace.

50

19 **than forever.**
Kaholo left.
Hands scoop down, cross,
and open above head.

20 **Promise me that you will leave me**
Ka'o right, left.
Hands from self,
then out to right side.

21 **never**
Kaholo right.
Left hand on hip,
right finger gesturing "never."

25 **the sun**
Dip as you kaholo left.
Shape the sun starting at the
knees and rise overhead.

26 **Blue skies of**
Kaholo right.
Hands cross above head and
open for the skies.

27 **Hawaii smile on**
Kaholo left.
Right hand up.
Left hand, palm up, show land
from right to left.

22 **Now that we are**
Kaholo left.
Arms outstretched and coming
together, palms up.

23 **one**
Ka'o right, left.
Clasp hands forward on right ka'o,
then at heart on left ka'o.

24 **Clouds won't hide**
Kaholo right.
Roll hands above head from left
to right.

28 **this our**
Step right, then left beginning to
move in a circle. Right hand at
chest, left hand up, alternating for
four counts.

29 **wedding day!**
Continue motions
to complete the circle.

30 **I do**
Kaholo right.
Hands at mouth and out.

31 **love you**
Kaholo left.
Love motion then point
to the left.

32 **With all my**
Kaholo right.
Left hand at heart, right hand
sweeps from side to bosom.

33 **heart**
Dipped ka'o, left, right two counts.
Roll hands at heart for two
counts.

37 **I will love you longer**
Kaholo right.
Hands to self,
then cross to embrace.
(same as step 18)

38 **than forever.**
Kaholo left.
Hands scoop down, cross, and
open above head.
(same as step 19)

39 **Promise me that you will
leave me**
Ka'o right, left.
Hands from self,
then out to right side.
(same as step 20)

34 **Here and**
Lele left, then lele right.
Right hand to chest,
left hand forward,
alternate hands on lele.
(same as step 15)

35 **now dear**
Kaholo left.
Open hands, palms up.
(same as step 16)

36 **All my love I vow dear**
'Ami four counts.
Hands outstretched and crossing
to embrace.
(same as step 17)

40 **never**
Kaholo right.
Left hand on hip,
right finger gesturing "never."
(same as step 21)

41 **Now that we are**
Kaholo left.
Arms outstretched and coming
together, palms up.
(same as step 22)

42 **one**
Ka'o right, left.
Clasp hands forward on right ka'o,
then at heart on left ka'o.
(same as step 23)

43 **Clouds won't hide**
Kaholo right.
Roll hands above head. from left to right.
(same as step 24)

44 **the sun**
Dip as you kaholo left.
Shape the sun starting at the knees and rise overhead.
(same as step 25)

45 **Blue skies of**
Kaholo right.
Hands cross above head and open for the skies.
(same as step 26)

49 **I do**
Kaholo right.
Hands at mouth and out.
(same as step 30)

50 **love you**
Kaholo left.
Love motion then point to the left.
(same as step 31)

51 **With all my**
Kaholo right.
Left hand at heart, right hand sweeps from side to bosom.
(same as step 32)

46 **Hawaii smile on**
Kaholo left.
Right hand up.
Left hand, palm up, show land
from right to left.
(same as step 27)

47 **this our**
Step right, then left beginning to
move in a circle. Right hand at
chest, left hand up, alternating for
four counts.
(same as step 28)

48 **wedding day!**
Continue motions
to complete the circle.
(same as step 29)

52 **heart**
Dipped ka'o, left, right two counts.
Roll hands at heart for two
counts.
(same step as 33)

53 **With all my**
Kaholo left.
Left hand at heart, right hand
sweeps from side to bosom.
(same as step 32)

54 **heart**
Dipped ka'o, right, left two counts.
Roll hands at heart for two
counts.
(same step as 33)

To complete song, step back on
left foot. Point right foot and bow.

Glossary

aloha — love, hello, goodbye
'ama 'ama — mullet
'auana — to dance freely
'awapuhi — ginger blossom
'okolehao — delicious drink
'opu — belly
ha'ina 'ia mai ana ka puana — "this is the story I tell"
halau — school
ho'omalimali — to flatter
huki — to pull
hukilau — pull fish nets in
hula — Hawaiian dance
kahiko — ancient
kama'aina — native-born
Kamehameha — referring to the king

kane — man, boy
kau kau — slang word for food
kou lima nani e — your lovely hands
kumu hula — hula teacher
La'ie Bay — North Shore on O'ahu
lau lau — food wrapped in taro leaves and tied in ti leaves
lei — garland of flowers
malihini — newcomer
pali — cliff
pau — finished
poi — pounded cooked taro
Waikiki — famous beach on O'ahu
wahine — woman, girl
wela ka hau — "have a good time"